SWEAR WORD
COLORING BOOK

THIS BOOK BELONG TO

"Life is like a rainbow.
You need both rain and sun
to make its colors appear."

Fuck Off

"Life is like a rainbow.
You need both rain and sun
to make its colors appear."

Bitch

"Life is like a rainbow.
You need both rain and sun
to make its colors appear."

I
Don't
Give
A
Damn

"Life is like a rainbow.
You need both rain and sun
to make its colors appear."

Bitch
Face

"Life is like a rainbow.
You need both rain and sun
to make its colors appear."

Calm the
fuck down!

"Life is like a rainbow.
You need both rain and sun
to make its colors appear."

Go to
Hell,
Bitch

"Life is like a rainbow.
You need both rain and sun
to make its colors appear."

Shut
the
FUCK
UP

"Life is like a rainbow.
You need both rain and sun
to make its colors appear."

Prick

"Life is like a rainbow.
You need both rain and sun
to make its colors appear."

You're
Such
a
dick!!

"Life is like a rainbow.
You need both rain and sun
to make its colors appear."

Dumbass

"Life is like a rainbow.
You need both rain and sun
to make its colors appear."

Piss
Off

"Life is like a rainbow.
You need both rain and sun
to make its colors appear."

Crap

"Life is like a rainbow.
You need both rain and sun
to make its colors appear."

Holy
Shit

"Life is like a rainbow.
You need both rain and sun
to make its colors appear."

Shitbag

"Life is like a rainbow.
You need both rain and sun
to make its colors appear."

Bollocks

"Life is like a rainbow.
You need both rain and sun
to make its colors appear."

Bastard

"Life is like a rainbow.
You need both rain and sun
to make its colors appear."

Pussy

"Life is like a rainbow.
You need both rain and sun
to make its colors appear."

Douche bag

"Life is like a rainbow.
You need both rain and sun
to make its colors appear."

ASSHAT

"Life is like a rainbow.
You need both rain and sun
to make its colors appear."

Screw You

"Life is like a rainbow.
You need both rain and sun
to make its colors appear."

FUCK!
FUCK! FUCK!
FUCK!

"Life is like a rainbow.
You need both rain and sun
to make its colors appear."

dickhead

"Life is like a rainbow.
You need both rain and sun
to make its colors appear."

DIPSHIT

"Life is like a rainbow.
You need both rain and sun
to make its colors appear."

fuck
Love

"Life is like a rainbow.
You need both rain and sun
to make its colors appear."

Asshole

"Life is like a rainbow.
You need both rain and sun
to make its colors appear."

Shit

"Life is like a rainbow.
You need both rain and sun
to make its colors appear."

Fuck
You

"Life is like a rainbow.
You need both rain and sun
to make its colors appear."

Fuck
off

9 781688 176188